Chadwick

Written by Shondra M. Quarles

Illustrated by Zuri Book Pros

LITERACY

@EYEHEARTLITERACY

SHONDRA M. QUARLES

Copyrighted Material
Chadwick
Copyright © 2021 by Shondra M. Quarles/Eye Heart Literacy, LLC/Ponchaveli. All Rights Reserved.
No part of this book may be reproduced or transmitted in any form or by any means, mechanical or electronic, including photocopying or recording, or by an information storage and retrieval system, or transmitted by
e-mail without permission in writing from the publisher, except for the inclusion of brief quotations in a review. This book is for entertainment purposes only. The views expressed are those of the author alone.

Front Cover Design by Ponchaveli Studios
Interior Design by Shondra M. Quarles unless otherwise credited

ISBN 978-1-7377009-9-9 (Paperback)

Printed in the United States of America
First printing edition 2021

Eye Heart Literacy, LLC
eyeheartliteracy@gmail.com
https://eyeheartliteracy.carrd.co/

I wrote this book in tribute to the legendary Chadwick A. Boseman. Chadwick was extremely loved, especially by children. He discovered early on that his purpose was brighter than entertainment, television, and film. How different would our world be if we all discovered our true purpose?

Thank you to the purpose-driven artists who shared their Chadwick Boseman-inspired artwork. Thank you, Maxwell Brittan, for sharing your tribute photo. Thank you, Lan Manuel Print House. Thank you, Taliah Gipson, for proofreading my manuscript. Thank you, Kelli Wooten, for the fan art layout idea. A special thank you to my cover model, Jonah B. A special thank you to Nuru Witherspoon at The Witherspoon Law Group http://thewitherspoonlawgroup.com/. You all helped make this tribute book a dream come true.

"You should rather find purpose than a job or a career. Purpose crosses disciplines. Purpose is an essential element of you. It is the reason you are on the planet at this particular time in history. Your very existence is wrapped up in things you are here to fulfill. Whatever you choose for a career path, remember the struggles along the way are only meant to shape you for your purpose."

~Chadwick A. Boseman

Chadwick Boseman was born in the state of South Carolina on November 29, 1976.

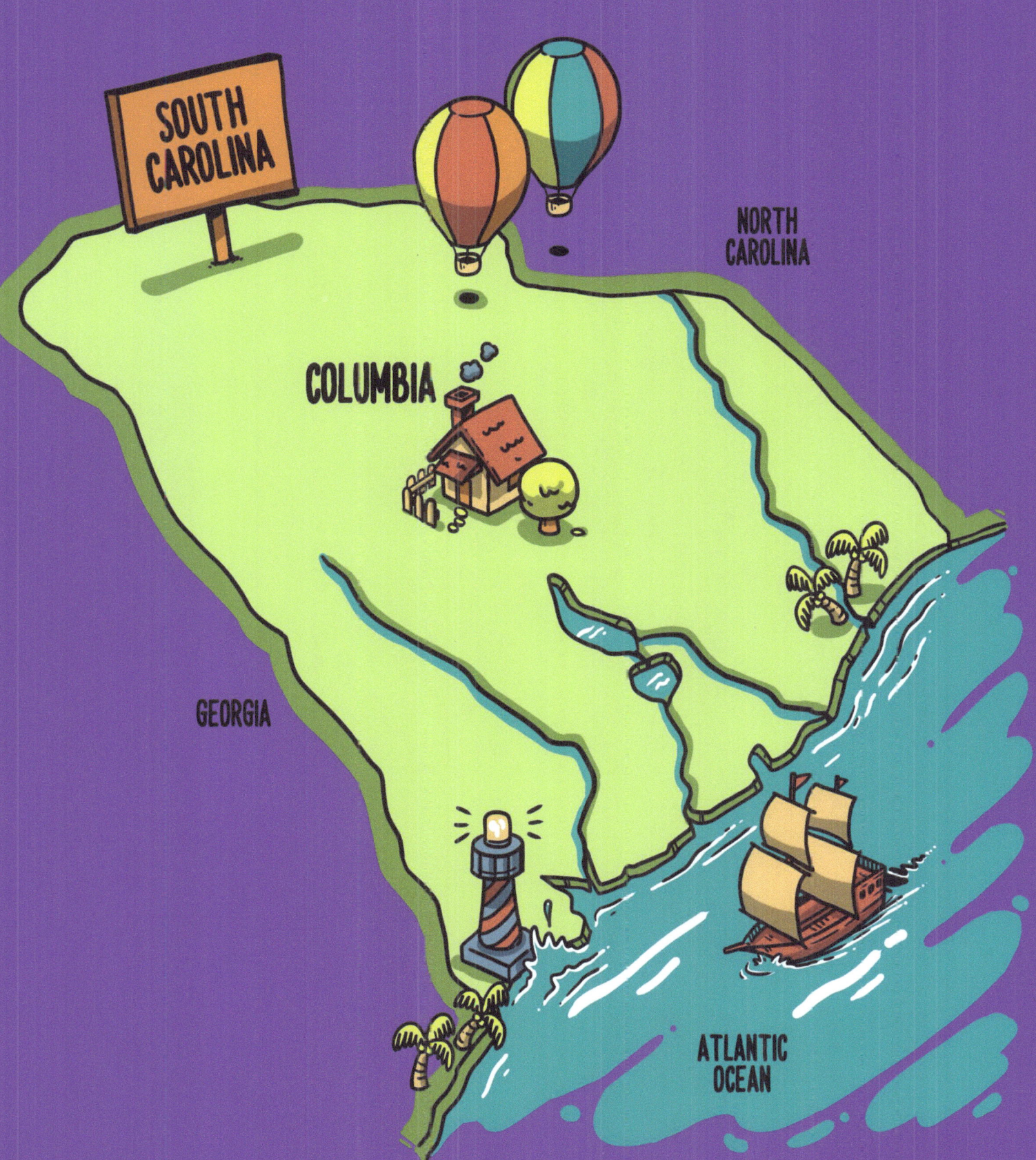

He grew up in a loving family who supported his big dreams.

After graduating from high school, Chadwick went to Howard University. One of his professors was actress Phylicia Rashad. She reached out to legendary actor Denzel Washington, who secretly paid for Chadwick to attend a summer acting program at Oxford University.

Chadwick was a powerful storyteller who took pride in the characters he played. He refused to play stereotypical roles based on how people looked or where they lived. He wanted to change the way Black people were seen on television and in movies.

In the movie, *42*, Chadwick taught us the history of Jackie Robinson. Jackie Robinson was the first African American, major league baseball player.

During the time Chadwick played Jackie Robinson, he was invited to the White House. He met with the first African American president, Barack Obama, and his wife, Michelle. Chadwick took part in the event to work with kids. He was a hero they looked up to.

Chadwick went on to play the Godfather of Soul, James Brown, in the movie *Get on Up*. James Brown had a unique voice and musical style. He was well known for his creative dance moves.

He later co-produced the movie, *Marshall,* as well as played Thurgood Marshall. Thurgood Marshall was a lawyer and civil rights activist who later became the first, African American Supreme Court Justice.

In the movie, *Black Panther*, Chadwick was a king who ruled Wakanda. In Wakanda, the people were Black, beautiful, and gifted. His starring role, as the first major Black superhero, would be one of his greatest performances. The movie was popular worldwide, and it gave Black children a chance to see a superhero who looked like them.

Although Chadwick earned many awards for his professional achievements, perhaps his greatest achievements were being a good son, kind brother,

loving husband,

and a real-life superhero to children around the world.

Chadwick lived his life with a plan that guided him. He also showed that if you follow your dreams and be kind, you can become a real-life superhero too.

Chadwick Forever!
November 29, 1976 – August 28, 2020

Maxwell Brittan
Photo by: Renita Purvis (Mom)
Instagram: @maxunlimited2013

GOLDEN GLOBE AWARD WINNER

Design idea by Shondra M. Quarles

Design idea by Shondra M. Quarles

Howard University officially renamed its fine arts building after Chadwick A. Boseman. His legacy will forever live on.

Artist Spotlight

We love you Chadwick Boseman!
(Digital Design: Kelli Wooten)

Artist: Ponchaveli
www.ponchaveli.com

Artist: Christopher "C-Ray" Rayson
www.c-rayart.com

Artist: Kamronbek Bohodirov
Instagram: artkamron
Email: bohodirkamron10@gmail.com

Instagram: @mellocat
Twitter: @mellocatart
https://mellocat.weebly.com/

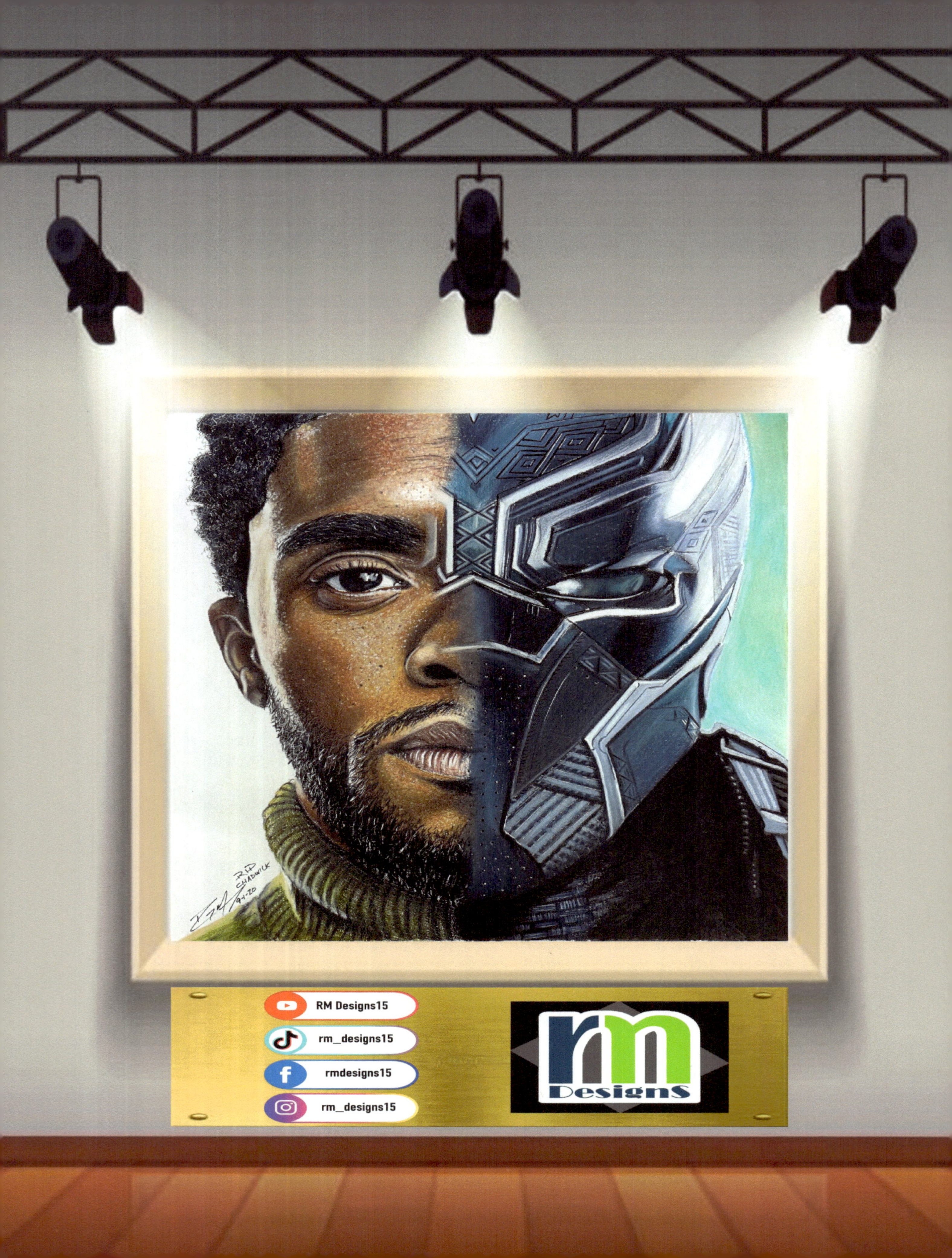
RM Designs15
rm_designs15
rmdesigns15
rm_designs15
rm
Designs

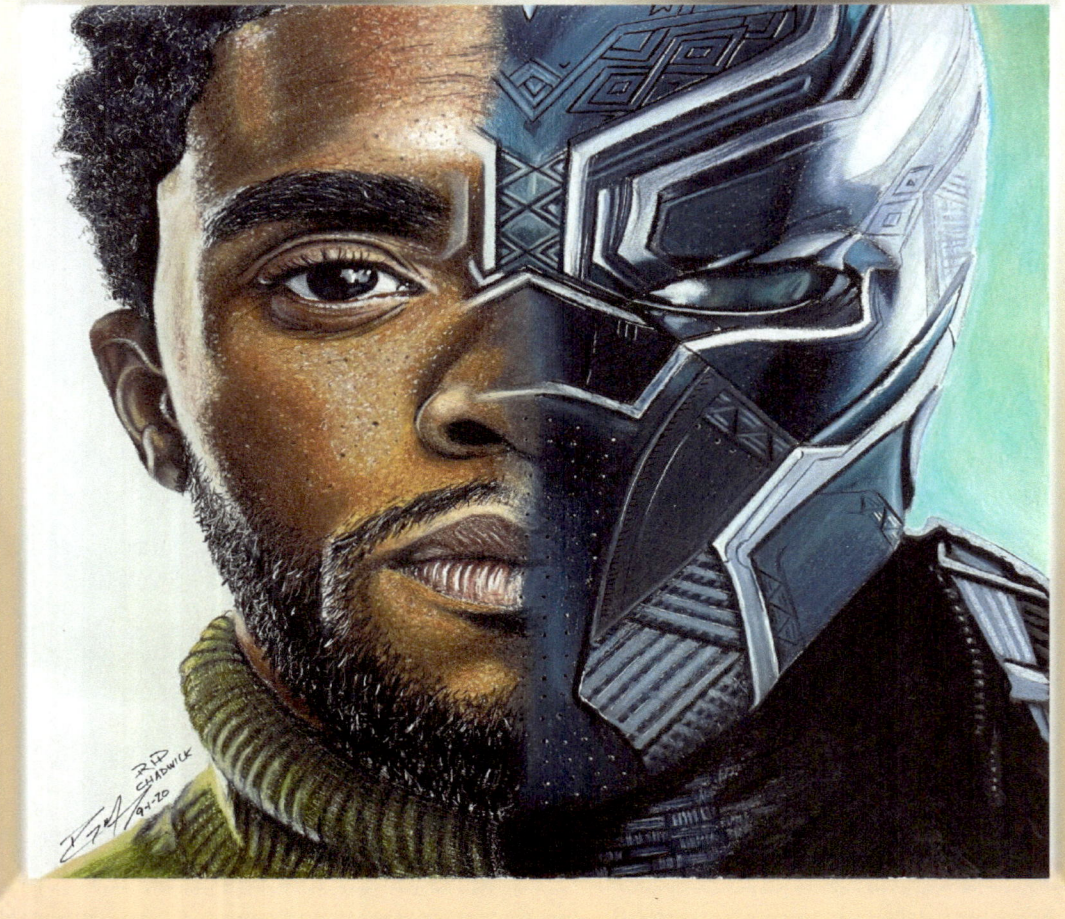

https://www.instagram.com/rowielin
Email: rowielin@gmail.com

Instagram.com/celestialnichole/
Twitter.com/celest_nichole/
etsy.com/shop/CelestialNichole

Instagram: @Tecnificent
Email: Tecnificent@gmail.com
www.Tecnificent.com

https://www.instagram.com/razzler_design/?hl=en
https://razzlerdesign.myportfolio.com/

Author Shondra M. Quarles
AS SEEN ON Master P Reviews EP 41